A Guide for Using

The Golden Goblet

in the Classroom

Based on the book written by Eloise Jarvis McGraw

*This guide written by **Mari Lu Robbins***

Teacher Created Materials, Inc.
6421 Industry Way
Westminster, CA 92683
www.teachercreated.com
©1995 Teacher Created Materials
Reprinted, 2001
Made in U.S.A.
ISBN 1-55734-442-6

Cover Art by
Keith Vasconcelles

Table of Contents

Introduction

What a wonderful gift it is to be able to read good books! With good books at hand we are never lonely, because they entertain, inspire, inform, and enrich our lives. Once found, a good book forever remains a loyal friend able to excite our imaginations.

In Literature Units, we take great care to choose those books that one can return time and time again for companionship and enlightenment.

Teachers using this literature unit will find the following features to supplement their own valuable ideas:

- Sample Lesson Plans

- Pre-reading Activities

- Biographical Sketch of the Author

- Book Summary

- Vocabulary Lists and Suggested Vocabulary Activities

- Chapters grouped for study, with each Section including:

    — a quiz

    — a hands-on project

    — a cooperative learning activity

    — a cross-curriculum connection

    — an extension into the reader's life

- Post-reading Activities

- Book Report Ideas

- Research Ideas

- Culminating Activity

- Three Different Options for Unit Tests

- Bibliography

- Answer Key

We welcome you to this unit, confident you will find it a valuable addition to your planning and teaching. Our goal is to help you inspire your students to a love for good books.

Sample Lesson Plan

Each of the lessons below can take from one to several days to complete.

LESSON 1
- Introduce and complete some or all of the pre-reading activities found on page 5.
- Read about the author with your students (page 6).
- Read the book summary with your students (page 7).
- Discuss the many gods and goddesses of ancient Egypt (page 45).
- Introduce the vocabulary list for Section 1 (page 8).

LESSON 2
- Read chapters 1 through 3. As you read, place the vocabulary words in the context of the story and discuss their meanings.
- Select a vocabulary activity (page 9).
- Build a pyramid (page 11).
- Make a timeline (page 12).
- Discuss the book in terms of geography (page 13).
- Begin readers' response journals (page 14).
- Administer the Section 1 quiz (page 10).
- Introduce the vocabulary list for Section 2 (page 8).

LESSON 3
- Read chapters 4 through 6. Place the vocabulary words in context and discuss their meanings.
- Select a vocabulary activity (page 9).
- Design a symbol for yourself (page 16).
- Create a code (page 17).
- Learn how hieroglyphics were decoded (page 18).
- Write a letter for help for Ranofer (page 19).
- Administer the Section 2 quiz (page 15).
- Introduce the vocabulary list for Section 3 (page 8).

LESSON 4
- Read chapters 7 through 9. Place the vocabulary words in context and discuss their meanings.
- Select a vocabulary activity (page 9).
- Make your own funerary mask (page 21).
- Discuss how Ranofer can reshape his life (page 22).
- Discuss the book in terms of history (page 23).

LESSON 4 *(cont)*
- Become an archaeologist (page 24).
- Administer the Section 3 quiz (page 20).
- Introduce the vocabulary list for Section 4 (page 8).

LESSON 5
- Read chapters 10 through 12. Place the vocabulary words in context and discuss their meanings.
- Select a vocabulary activity (page 9).
- Make Egyptian jewelry (page 26).
- Demonstrate how mummies were made (page 27).
- Discuss book in terms of math (page 28).
- Write a story about the mummy's curse (page 29).
- Administer the Section 4 quiz (page 25).
- Introduce the vocabulary list for Section 5 (page 8).

LESSON 6
- Read chapters 13 through 16. Place the vocabulary words in context and discuss their meanings.
- Select a vocabulary activity (page 9).
- Decorate your tomb (page 31).
- Prepare a time capsule (page 32).
- Learn to write dialogue (page 33).
- Make a decision (page 34).
- Administer the Section 5 quiz (page 30).

LESSON 7
- Discuss any questions your students may have about the story (page 35).
- Assign book report and research projects (pages 36 and 37).
- Begin work on the culminating activity (pages 38, 39 and 40).

LESSON 8
- Administer unit tests 1, 2 and/or 3 (pages 41, 42 and 43).
- Discuss the test answers and responses
- Discuss the students' opinions and enjoyment of the book.
- Provide a list of related reading for the students (page 46).

LESSON 9
- Celebrate the Festival of the Nile culminating activity (pages 38–40).

Before the Book

Before reading *The Golden Goblet,* completing some pre-reading activities will help your students get a feel for the time period and cultural framework in which the book is set. The ideas below will help students focus on the book and learn some fascinating information about a unique period in history.

1. Predict what the story might be about by hearing the title.

2. Predict what the story might be about by looking at the cover illustration.

3. Discuss historical fiction.

4. Individually, or in small groups, write brief, fictionalized accounts about important events in your country's history.

5. Discuss ancient Egypt and what the students already know about it. Students may be amazed to learn that historical Egypt began about 5,000 years ago when the pharaoh, Menes, first united Upper and Lower Egypt and built his new capital, Memphis. It was probably in Memphis that the unique religion and way of life which we associate with ancient Egypt began.

6. Discuss the idea of reincarnation and what effect a belief in reincarnation might have on a people who truly believed they would live forever.

7. Describe the gods in "Gods and Goddesses of Ancient Egypt" on page 45, and discuss how each may have affected the lives of ordinary Egyptians.

8. Answer these questions:

   • What would it be like if:

     — most boys and girls did not go to school?

     — you had to live with someone who was cruel to you and gave you no choices?

     — you had to earn your own living now?

     — you learned that someone you depended on was using you to steal?

     — you knew you would be treated harshly and punished as an adult if someone thought you were committing a serious crime?

   • Write a paragraph describing how you feel about one of these questions.

About the Author

Eloise McGraw began writing at the age of eight and has not stopped since, except for the ten years she spent in painting and drawing. Born in Houston in 1915 to Loy Hamilton, a merchant, and Genevieve Scoffern Jarvis, Eloise attended Principia College, where she received her BA in 1937. She also attended Oklahoma University and Colorado University and did graduate study in painting and sculpture. She became an instructor of portrait and figure painting, but her love is writing. On January 1, 1940, she married William Corbin McGraw, a writer and filbert grower. She has lived in Oregon for the past thirty-odd years.

Many of her books have won awards. *Crown Fire* was an honor book for the *New York Herald-Tribune's Childrens' Book Festival.* In 1952 she was runner-up for the Newbery Award with *Moccasin Trail,* and again for *The Golden Goblet* in 1962. She was awarded the Lewis Carroll Shelf Award in 1963. She has written many other books, including *Mara, Daughter of the Nile, Pharaoh,* and four teenage novels. She has been a contributor to *Jack and Jill, Childcraft, Parents' Magazine,* and *Writer.*

A woman of many interests, Eloise McGraw still enjoys painting and drawing, and she has illustrated the covers of some of her books. She also likes dancing, acting, puppetry, ceramics, horseback riding, and, of course, ancient Egypt. A dressmaker and bread baker, Mrs. McGraw also spends some of her spare time making woodcuts and wood engravings. In addition, she is a gourmet cook.

Mr. McGraw is also a writer of children's books, and together the McGraws travel as extensively as they can. These travels provide much of the information which forms the settings for Mrs. McGraw's books. In 1985 the McGraws visited the Bayeux tapestry in France, and that became the inspiration for her latest book, *The Striped Ships,* which is about the Norman Invasion into England. She also has been an enthusiastic visitor to Egypt, the setting of *The Golden Goblet.*

The Golden Goblet

by Eloise Jarvis McGraw

(Puffin Books, 1986)

(Available in Canada from Penguin; in UK from Penguin UK; and in AUS from Penguin Aus)

Ranofer was the son of a goldsmith who was famous for the beautiful jewelry and other luxuries made of pure gold which the Egyptian pharaohs and their queens loved, and for which he was paid well. That should have made life easy for Ranofer, especially in a land where a boy usually went on to become what his father was. As a small child he eagerly watched his father fashion lovely, intricate necklaces, bracelets, daggers, and tableware from the lustrous metal. Ranofer's dream was to become an apprentice to Zau, the great goldsmith, so that one day he, too, would be famous and wealthy like his father.

But it seemed fate had determined otherwise for Ranofer when his beloved father died, and he was forced to live with his cruel and evil half-brother, Gebu.

Gebu beat Ranofer at the slightest excuse and gave him only the food left over from his own meals. Ranofer was forced to sleep outside under a tree. While he was allowed to work in a goldsmith's workshop, it was only as a laborer, sweeping up after the gold workers and running errands, because Gebu would not pay the fee required for an apprenticeship. It seemed that Ranofer could never escape, and then things began to happen.

First, Ranofer discovered Gebu was using him to steal gold which was intended for the pharaoh's tomb. Then Gebu took Ranofer away from the gold workshop he loved and forced him to apprentice as a stonecutter. Ranofer's life became more wretched than ever, except for two friends he had made.

When Ranofer discovered that Gebu was stealing from the pharaohs, he feared for his own life, because the penalty for such a crime was death. How could he stop this horrible crime without being charged for it himself? How could justice be brought to the evil Gebu? With his friends, Heqet and the Ancient, Ranofer planned how to bring about the downfall of Gebu.

The Golden Goblet will keep you on the edge of your seat, hoping to see right prevail and evil overthrown. It is truly an adventure of the best kind, set in the glorious days of the pharaohs and the building of the Valley of the Kings.

Vocabulary Lists

SECTION 1
Chapters 1–3

molten	crucible	hollowed
ingot	urchin	splendid
amulet	beneficent	intensity
illustrious	apprentice	diminish
anneal	ingratiating	sibilant
servility	insolent	ferment
plague	artisan	treachery
puny	jubilant	ebony
destine	surly	brusque
ailing	vague	debris
access	angular	guttural
jocular	meander	papyrus
extricate	countenance	aghast
speculative	ingrate	cower

SECTION 2
Chapters 4–6

scrupulous	funerary	wraithlike
indifferent	irascible	designate
yonder	devise	glib
snippet	involuntary	cranny
wheedle	preemptory	metallic
endure	raucous	joviality
ostensible	pretext	destitute
natron	rapture	obsequious
incredible	venomous	obscure
sarcophagus	alabaster	chisel
gnarled	awry	mutilate
authoritative	disdain	disconsolate
inert	interminable	descend
respite	conspicuous	malevolent

SECTION 3
Chapters 7–9

accordance	scythe	desiccate
eke	menial	contemptuous
foreman	foliage	subdue
improbable	ragamuffin	diffident
entice	nauseate	anise
philosophical	trough	hauteur
barter	voluminous	gravely
ritual	depression	dismal
drover	craft	earnest
persuade	pervade	austere
intrusion	recriminate	wrought
diligence	audible	scrutinize
flounder	arrogant	creditable
ridicule	alter	dubious

SECTION 4
Chapters 10–12

precarious	grope	scroll
intermittent	exasperate	endure
conjure	phantom	reverberate
nocturnal	fiasco	truncate
impudent	tedious	mongrel
sulky	confer	temerity
audacious	barque	whet
radiance	exquisite	hieroglyph
inscription	sufficient	adder
scarab	seal	tinder
kindle	venture	laden
laconic	ravenous	rivet
conspiratorial	morose	abstracted
astound	bewilder	viper

SECTION 5
Chapters 13–16

crevice	crude	plait	futile	simultaneous	conviction
skeptical	sentry	ominous	citadel	desolate	intensify
consternation	vengeful	guttural	necropolis	apprehensive	involuntary
projection	vengeance	scan	serenity	excavate	ventilate
courtier	sanctuary	palanquin	eloquent	cumbersome	homage
chariot	acute	wager	pillage	eavesdrop	obliterate
villain	embark	slacken	desecrate	retinue	brandish

Vocabulary Activity Ideas

A list of vocabulary words is included for each section. Divide and assign words to students in the most appropriate way for your class. Always discuss the words in terms of the meanings used in *The Golden Goblet*.

Using the vocabulary words in a variety of activities will help students remember and understand them. Try the activities below which seem most appropriate for your students.

Charades — Ask each student to choose one word and act it out for the class.

Write a Story — Choose several words from the vocabulary list, and have the students write a short story using those words.

Fill in the Blank — Give the students a paragraph in which a number of words has been left out. They then fill each blank with the missing word.

Crossword Clues — Make a crossword puzzle with several of the words filled in and numbered. The students then provide the clues based on the definitions of the words.

Vocabulary Bingo — On a card with twenty-five spaces, students randomly write a vocabulary word in each space except the free middle space. A caller reads definitions and the students mark correct words. The first one to cover a row, column or diagonal wins.

True or False — Present the students with a number of sentences containing vocabulary words. The students use true or false to indicate whether the word is used correctly.

Word Search — Have students make word search puzzles with definitions for clues.

Go Fishing — Vocabulary words are written on slips of paper and put into a container. Each student "fishes" for one word, looks it up, and then reports back to the class on the meaning of the word. Students record the meanings into individual or class dictionaries.

Words of the Day — Write several words on the board before students enter the classroom. As a warm-up activity, students use a dictionary to look up the definitions. Each word is defined orally for the class, then the definition's written on chart paper or on the board. Students write the definitions in notebooks or individual dictionaries for study.

Categories — Place a number of words on the board. Each word is then put into a list according to whether it is a noun, verb or adjective. As each word is placed into a list, discuss why that word goes into that list rather than another and why it is important to see the word within the context of the story.

Draw the Word — Draw a picture or cartoon showing the definition of the word being pictured or in some way acted out. In this activity, a silly portrayal may put a little fun into vocabulary study.

Quiz Time!

1. On the back of this paper, list three important events in Section 1.

2. Who was Ranofer's father, and what was his occupation? _____

    _____

3. In what city did Ranofer live? _____

4. Why did Ranofer dislike Ibni so much? _____

    _____

5. Ranofer and the people he knows use many expressions which are new to you. Why do you think this is so? _____

    _____

    _____

6. List at least three ways in which Gebu mistreats Ranofer. _____

    _____

    _____

7. What had Ranofer learned to do which was very unusual for boys of his time?

    _____

    _____

8. How does Heqet show his friendship for Ranofer?_____

    _____

    _____

9. What does Rekh ask Ranofer to do? _____

    _____

10. On the back of this paper, explain what Gebu meant when he said, "I must have some use of you."

Build a Pyramid

The ancient Egyptians believed in a life after death. This belief was so strong that it dominated their lives and their culture for many centuries. During Ranofer's time, the life and work of all the people centered around the building and furnishing of the tombs for the pharaohs and other important people.

The most famous of these tombs, because they are still standing after 5,000 years, are the great pyramids. The earliest pyramids were called step pyramids because, as their name suggests, they had steps up their sides. When these pyramids were built, it was believed that the dead king's spirit could climb the steps to join the sun god at the top. Later, the pyramids were faced with smooth, white limestone. Only one of them still has part of the limestone facing remaining.

The pyramids of Egypt are the only thing still standing of the Seven Wonders of the Ancient World and are now part of the Seven Wonders of the Modern World. More than 87 pyramids still exist.

Activity

There are several materials you can use to build a model pyramid, including sugar cubes, and handmade clay blocks. Choose the material which is easily available to you, and build a pyramid of your own. Remember:

1. The base of the pyramid is absolutely square, so the shape of the bottom of your pyramid will have four equal sides and four right angles.

2. The pyramid should be approximately two-thirds as high as each side is wide.

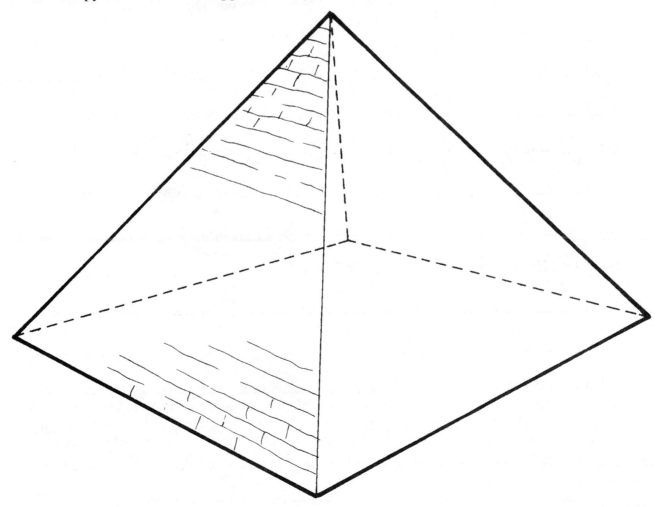

Make a Timeline

It is hard to imagine just how long ago the Egyptians began building their civilization and the marvelous tombs and temples which have lasted for thousands of years. Putting a timeline up around the walls of your classroom may help you visualize the passage of time more clearly. We don't know for certain how long man was on earth before the Egyptian society, so when you finish your timeline, remember that man probably was here at least 90,000 years before your timeline begins, and the earth, itself, many millions of years before man!

Activity

Divide into groups of four or five. Before you actually begin making your timeline, you need to make some decisions.

First, measure the distance you have to work with. Can you go all the way around the room, across one wall, or an even shorter distance? After determining the distance you have, calculate how many centuries have passed since ten thousand years B.C. and what distance, given the total length you have to work with, you can allot to each century. Give each century an equal amount of space on your timeline. Use computer paper, sheets of paper taped together, or rolled paper for your timeline.

1. Beginning with the year 10,000 B.C., mark the centuries on your paper up to the present time.
2. Fill in the following information in appropriate spaces on your timeline:

10,000-5,000 B.C. The first villages grow on the banks of the Nile.

3,100 B.C. Menes unites Upper and Lower Egypt and becomes the first pharaoh. He establishes his capital at Memphis.

2,630 B.C. The first step pyramid is built at Saqqara.

2,575 B.C. Bronze replaces copper, and the pyramids of Giza are built. Bodies are first embalmed. This time is known as the Old Kingdom.

2,134 B.C. The Old Kingdom ends because of power struggles and Egypt is divided.

2,040 B.C. The Middle Kingdom begins and Egypt is reunited with Thebes as its capital

1,640 B.C. The Middle Kingdom ends.

1,550 B.C. New Kingdom begins, Egypt has its first woman ruler who built Dier el Bahari as a monument to herself, and an army is established.

1,400 B.C. Egypt reaches the height of its power under Thutmose III.

1,070 B.C. Egypt begins to lose its power.

661 B.C. The Assyrians sack Thebes.

332 B.C. Alexander the Great conquers Egypt.

51 B.C. Cleopatra rules Egypt.

30 B.C. Rome conquers Egypt and makes it a province.

To make your timeline really interesting, include on it some more modern historical facts such as when we started marking time as A.D., the first printing press, the American Revolution, the invention of the locomotive, automobile, airplane, television, and the personal computer. How about your own birthday and those of your parents and grandparents? Make your timeline as interesting and inclusive as you can, and by all means, decorate it!

The Gift of the Nile

Ancient Egypt, one of the most highly developed of ancient civilizations, could not have developed except for the Nile River. All great civilizations of the past were built near water, for people need water for their very lives, and Egypt was no exception. Without the Nile, Egypt could not have existed at all because it gets no rain. No crops would have grown, and life would have been impossible. Egypt would have stayed nothing but desert forever.

Every year the Nile floods its banks, leaving behind a rich, dark soil in which plants grow easily. This river valley is called the Black Land because of the color of the soil, and this is where the towns and villages were built as well as the great cities like Memphis and Thebes. The Black Land spreads out from the Nile in only two places: at the Nile Valley Delta and at the Faiyum, an oasis south of Memphis which is linked to the Nile. Both of these places are fertile and crowded. Only desert nomads and wild animals dared to roam the Red Land, as the Egyptian desert surrounding the Black Land was called.

The Egyptians buried their dead in the western desert. All of the great tombs, including the pyramids, Dier el Bahari, and the Valley of the Kings, are located in the western desert. This practice of burying their dead in the desert probably had something to do with the growth of their belief in life forever, because bodies would have been mummified naturally in the dry sand.

At its north end the Nile empties into the Mediterranean Sea through the Delta, and trading ships have long come that way from other parts of the world. It was only a little over a century ago, however, that a lengthy international search finally traced the source of the Nile to Lake Victoria.

Activity

On the map, color the banks of the Nile green, the Delta and the Faiyum south of Memphis green, the surrounding desert orange, and the water blue. Use another map to locate the pyramids and sphinx and add them to your map.

Readers' Response Journals

Competent readers become totally involved in their reading. They actually live vicariously the events in a good book just as though they were taking part themselves. They imagine, they ponder, and they project their own feelings and experiences into what they read, and in doing so, they become meaning-makers. Readers' response journals provide a wonderful means to help your students improve their meaning-making ability and at the same time increase their comprehension by helping them to respond to the events, characters, and time period of a story. Here are some ideas for making your students' journals an effective meaning-making process for them.

- Tell your students that the journals are intended to allow them a structured space in which to record their feelings, thoughts, ideas, questions, and reactions to what they read.

- Provide your students with questions, such as the ones on page 44, or definite guidelines as to what they will respond to in their journals each day. Give the day's question before the reading, so students may mull over it as they read. Structuring the reading in this way will help your students retain more of what they read by helping them stay focused.

- Allow the students to use the journal assignments as practice for more formal writing, like tests or essays. For example, on one day ask a question to which the student will reply as though writing an autobiographical incident while pretending to be a character from the book. On another day, ask a question that asks for speculation about causes and effects, or one which asks for a solution to the problem a character is having in the story.

- Give students time to write in their journals daily. Stress to them that they will not be graded on what they write, but that they will receive credit on their final grade for the care and effort they direct toward the journals.

Write positive, but truthful, comments to the students occasionally, letting them know you are reading and enjoying how they are responding to the book.

Allow voluntary sharing of something a student has written in the journal.

If it is possible to store the journals in the classroom, they will always be available and will remain neater than if they are carried around. This will also communicate to the students the importance you place on them as a learning tool.

Quiz Time!

1. On the back of this paper list three important events from Section 2.

2. Who is Rekh?_____

3. Why does Ranofer decide to trust Heqet? _____

    _____

4. How did Ibni steal the gold for Gebu? _____

    _____

5. How did Rekh find out about the gold thefts, and what did he do about them?

    _____

6. What was the penalty for stealing from the tombs? _____

    _____

7. Pretending to be Gebu, describe your young half–brother, Ranofer. _____

    _____

    _____

8. How did Gebu punish Ranofer when Ibni was no longer at the gold shop?

    _____

    _____

9. What did Ranofer notice about the old man's hands?_____

    _____

10. What do you think will happen to Ranofer if he stays long in the stonecutting shop?

    _____

    _____

Man, the Symbol-Maker

A unique quality of man is his ability to make symbols. Man uses signs, words, or objects to stand for something other than what those signs, words, or objects actually are. We all recognize what certain symbols mean. For example, the symbol "+" tells us that we are able to add two or more numbers together, and "?" means a question is being asked.

The Egyptians had many symbols. The mirror case on the right was made in the form of a common Egyptian symbol, the *ankh*. This was the hieroglyphic sign for "life."

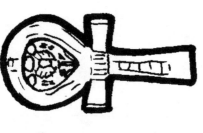

Cartouche is a French name given to the oval rings in which a pharaoh's name and the names of other members of the royal family were written. In a cartouche, the personal name of the pharaoh might be followed by a saying about him. The Egyptians called the cartouche a *shenu*, which meant "to encircle," because they believed the pharaoh ruled all that the sun encircled. The cartouche also stood for infinity.

The Rosetta Stone contained six cartouches spaced at regular intervals and all enclosing the same hieroglyphic signs written in the same order, and this was what gave scholars their first clue to help them decipher the code.

Activity

Inside the cartouche to the right, design a symbol for yourself. Using symbols of your own, write something about yourself which tells who you are and why you are important. Decorate your cartouche, using bright colors and interesting designs.

16

Create a Code

All language is a way people have developed over many centuries to organize spoken sounds to express ideas. Not all language is written. Written language is created when man converts the words and ideas he speaks into symbols which can be seen. All written language is made up of symbols, but not all languages are written in the same set of symbols, or code. Many different codes, or systems for writing language, have been developed over the years, most of them based either on sounds or on pictures.

Modern English and other European languages, as well as Vietnamese and Indonesian, are based on the Roman alphabet. The Russian language is written with the Cyrillic alphabet, the language of India is written with the Hindi alphabet, and Chinese languages are written with pictograms.

When Jean-Francois Champollion decoded hieroglyphics, he was able to do it by comparing what he knew with what he didn't know until he found some matches, as in this illustration.

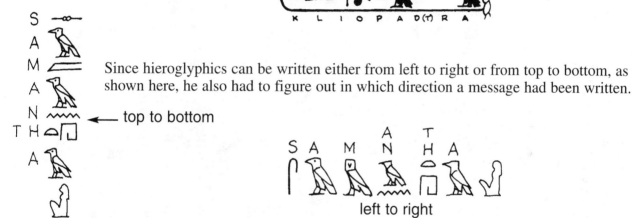

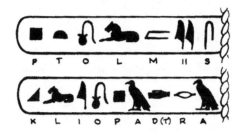

Since hieroglyphics can be written either from left to right or from top to bottom, as shown here, he also had to figure out in which direction a message had been written.

← top to bottom

left to right

Activity

In groups of three or four, invent a code of your own. Decide what your symbols will be based on—sounds, pictures, or even the Roman alphabet—and write a message to the class. Can you decode (figure out) the message below?

HINT: 👤 = n 🌲 = L ✏️ = a

Cracking the Code of Hieroglyphics

After Egypt became a part of the Roman Empire in 30 A.D., the people began to worship new gods and live new lifestyles based on the Roman way of life, and no one was able to read the ancient Egyptian form of writing called hieroglyphics for over 1600 years. Sand slowly covered the old temples and palaces, and Egypt became a place of mystery to outsiders. Then, in the 18th century, people again became interested in the fabulous civilization which had flourished there, and archaeologists began to dig up the ruins.

The first archaeologists to investigate the old temples and tombs were not interested in history, however. They wanted to find treasure, and they did much damage to the buildings which they ransacked, even breaking through seals with battering rams. Many of the ancient pieces, some of them huge, were taken from Egypt to faraway places in Europe, where they now may be seen in museums. Eventually this sort of violation of historic places became controlled, and a more scientific study of Egypt was begun.

The visitors to the ruins were amazed at the beautiful art work and writing on the walls of the tombs, the sarcophagi, and the beautiful implements they found. But just as visitors to other ancient civilizations have been puzzled as to what the ancient writing they found meant, so it was with the hieroglyphics. What could these fascinating symbols mean? Many of the symbols were pictographic, that is, picture writing, but what the symbols stood for had long been forgotten.

Then in 1700 some French soldiers made a remarkable discovery near Alexandria. They found a large black stone with a flat face on which had been written an inscription in three different forms of writing: Greek and two different kinds of Egyptian writing, including hieroglyphic.

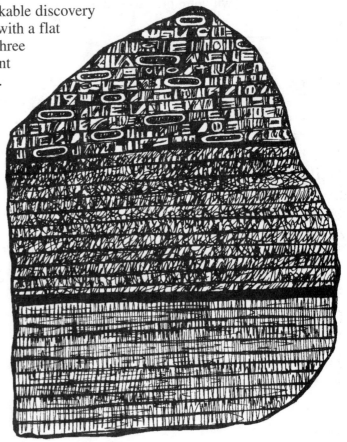

Using his knowledge of Greek, a French soldier named Jean-Francois Champollion studied the stone, comparing the Greek with the hieroglyphics. It took him 14 years to decipher his first word, "Ptolemy," the name of the Greeks who ruled as pharaohs for 300 years. By comparing the letters in Ptolemy with the spelling of Cleopatra, he was able to work out the symbols for the letters "p," "l," and "o," and begin cracking the code. Fortunately, the message in the inscriptions were identical so one could be used to learn the other.

The Rosetta Stone is now in the British Museum in London, where many thousands of visitors see it each year. An exact replica of the stone is also in the Rosicrucian Egyptian Museum in San Jose, California, and is regularly visited by students from many different schools.

Write a Letter for Help

Imagine that you are Ranofer living with Gebu. You are very unhappy, and you need to confide in someone, but it is very hard to trust others. If Gebu finds out what you're thinking, he will probably beat you even more, but you feel you just have to get out of your system all the pain and anger you're feeling. Heqet and the Ancient are the only friends you have, but even with them you have a lot of trouble expressing yourself out loud. Sometimes it is easier to write what we feel than to say it. In the space below, write a letter to either Heqet or the Ancient, telling them what Gebu is doing to you and how you feel about it.

Quiz Time!

1. On the back of this paper list three important events from Section 3.

2. What is made in the stonecutting shop? _____

    _____

3. How did Ranofer describe the stonecutting shop to Heqet? _____

    _____

4. Why does Heqet say that Ranofer has too much pride? _____

    _____

5. Why does the Ancient think Ranofer is silly for not wanting to be a stonecutter's

    apprentice? _____

    _____

6. Where does Ranofer go with Heqet?_____

    _____

7. How does Zau feel about Ranofer and about Ranofer's father? _____

    _____

8. What happened to Ranofer when he forgot his coppers? _____

    _____

9. What does Ranofer suddenly realize Gebu has been doing?_____

    _____

10. What do Ranofer, Heqet, and the Ancient plot together? _____

    _____

    _____

Make Your Mask

Of all the wonderful things found in the tomb of Tutankhamen, the most famous is the funerary mask which was placed directly over the mummy wrappings, and which was intended to look like the dead pharaoh. It's impossible, of course, to know whether or not the mask looked exactly like Tutankhamen, but the shape of the nose, lips, and chin all agree with the features which can be seen on his mummy.

This lovely work of art is truly incredible. It is made of solid gold $\frac{1}{8}$ inch (.3 cm) thick and is inlaid with lapis lazuli, carnelian, dark blue faience, and translucent quartz, and the eyes are made of obsidian. The goldsmith who created the mask certainly was a master artisan. It's no small wonder Ranofer wanted to be a goldsmith like his father. Indeed, maybe he was the one who, after he was a man, fashioned the mask for Tutankhamen, for Ranofer lived during the same Egyptian era as Tutankhamen.

You can make a mask for yourself. It won't be real gold, for who can afford to use real gold for such a thing now! But you can make one of papíer-mâché and paint it to look like gold.

Materials:

- Large tray, greased on the bottom

- Strips of newspaper or paper towels

- Wallpaper paste

- Objects such as paper cups, pieces of cardboard, spools, egg carton cups, or tissue spools suitable for forming features

- Paint in gold, royal blue, red, turquoise and black

- Acrylic spray for shine (Use only under supervision of an adult!)

Directions:

1. On the greased bottom of an upturned tray, apply two layers of paper strips. Let dry.

2. Use a variety of materials to shape features which will stand out, such as, nose, eyes, chin, ears, etc.

3. Cover with additional layers of papíer-mâché. Let dry.

4. Remove tray, and paint your mask.

5. Near the bottom of the mask, write in words or pictographs a statement or two about yourself which tells who you are and why you are important to the world.

Note: Try to make your mask look as much like you as possible. It may help to keep a photograph of yourself in front of you as you work.

Reshape Ranofer's Life

Ranofer goes with Heqet to the shop of Zau, the great goldsmith. Zau had been the friend of Ranofer's father, Thutra, and Ranofer hopes that Zau will solve his problems with Gebu by teaching him to be a goldsmith, too. However, when Zau tells Ranofer to dissolve his apprenticeship with Gebu so he can become a pupil of Zau's, Ranofer replies that if he did, Gebu would kill him. Ranofer desperately wants to become a pupil of Zau's, yet he cannot bring himself to do what he must do in order to become what he wants to be.

In addition, there are the problems of Gebu's thievery and his cruelty to Ranofer. Ranofer's life is in a very frustrating and painful state, but Zau plants a seed in Ranofer's mind when he says, *"It is clear that I can do nothing for you at the present. You must reshape your life into some other form. When you have done this, come to me and I will teach you."*

Activity

This is a chance for you to brainstorm your best ideas and come up with a plan to help Ranofer reshape his life and become what he wants to be. Until now, he has seen himself as a helpless victim, unable to do anything about his problems.

In groups of four or five, brainstorm a plan for Ranofer to reshape his life. List the possible answers you can think of for these questions:

- Must Ranofer remain a victim?

  _____

  _____

- How can Ranofer solve the problem of being beaten by Gebu?

  _____

  _____

- How can Ranofer leave the stonecutting shop and become Zau's pupil?

  _____

  _____

- What should Ranofer do with the knowledge that Gebu is a thief?

  _____

  _____

Come back together as a class for five to ten minutes and share the solutions you have considered with the rest of the class.

Who Was King Tut?

King Tutankhamen, sometimes referred to as "King Tut" for short, is probably for us the most famous of all the pharaohs. Although he was not a particularly important king, we know more about him than about other pharaohs from the wonderful things found in his tomb by Howard Carter. We know that he reigned from about 1334 B.C. to 1325 B.C. and that he was only eighteen or nineteen years old when he died, so he became king when he was only nine years old.

Tutankhamen was probably the son of the pharaoh Akhenaton and one of his minor wives. Men often married more than one woman in those days. We do know that he was not the son of Akhenaton's queen, Nefertiti, who had only daughters.

When he was still a child, Tutankhamen was married to Ankhesenpaaton, the daughter of Akhenaton and Nefertiti. In other words, he was probably married to his half-sister. Marrying sisters was a common practice among the pharaohs, because in this way the family was assured that it would maintain power. Also, there was a belief that the sun god shone only on the pharaoh, and marrying within the family kept this power of the god in the family. Two mummified babies found in the tomb were probably the children of Tutahkhamen and Ankhesenpaaton.

Tutankhamen's father, Akhenaton, sometimes called the "heretic king" by his enemies, was a very interesting pharaoh. He literally turned Egyptian society upside down during his rule when he decreed that rather than worshipping many gods, only Aton, the sun god, was to be worshipped and that Akhenaton was the only earthly intermediary for Aton. He built a new capital about two hundred miles (322 km) north of Thebes at Amarna where Tutankhamen was raised. As you can imagine, the priests of the temples, who had become very powerful over the centuries, were very upset at the loss of their power. Although Akhenaton ruled for seventeen years, the common people seem to have held onto their old beliefs. Tutankhamen was raised in the new religion, but he does not appear to have cared too much one way or the other which god or gods were worshipped, and during his reign, the old priesthoods again rose in importance.

The time during which Tutankhamen lived was a glorious time for Egypt. The land had become very wealthy and powerful. Great feasts in honor of Amon were held, and great temples were built. The Egyptian army ruled in parts of Asia, and old texts indicate that the temples were filled with many male and female slaves captured from abroad. The pharaoh was shown in pictures as vanquishing Egypt's foes, and although he apparently enjoyed archery, he did not actually go to battle. Tutankhamen died mysteriously. There was some damage to his skull, but it's not known whether this happened before or after his death, since his mummy was not in very good condition.

Activity: Research what you can learn about Akhenaton or his queen, Nefertiti, and write a brief report of what you learn. Share your findings with the class.

You, the Archaeologist

In October, 1922, Howard Carter was almost out of time. He had been working for fifteen years to find the tomb of King Tutankhamen in the Valley of the Kings. True, he had found a few small items—a faience cup bearing the pharaoh's name, pieces of gold foil with pictures and inscriptions of Tutankhamen and his wife, and a set of pottery canopic jars bearing the pharaoh's seal—but no major finds had been made by anyone for many years. Tomb robbers long ago seemed to have taken everything of value from the valley. In two months the money to pay for the project would run out, and he would have to give up.

Then, in early November, in a place he had thought could not be the right place, his workmen found the beginning of a staircase under a hut in front of the tomb of Ramses VI. Working very carefully, they cleared the stairway, and a door appeared. The door was sealed with the seals of the royal necropolis, the jackal god Anubis standing above nine defeated enemies. Could this be it? After all this time?

When the door was finally opened, a passageway was revealed which had been cut through bedrock and filled with rubble. Carter observed that it had been entered and then refilled many years before. That passage was cleared for twenty-five feet (8 m) from the entrance, and another sealed doorway was found. Carter drilled a small hole in the upper left-hand corner of the door and inserted a candle, and as his eyes adjusted to the gloom, an image of strange animals, statues, and shining gold emerged.

The antechamber looked like a junk store, but what wonderful junk: three ceremonial beds, thrones, vases, chariots, inlaid boxes, statuettes, weapons and many more luxurious items lying in heaps. The tomb had been ransacked soon after the burial, and jewels, gold and the burial oils had been taken, but since that time, no one had entered, and thousands of exquisitely beautiful things remained in the four rooms of the tomb. The burial chamber itself was filled with gold, and inside nested three coffins. One was made of solid gold and held the mummified body of King Tutankhamen! The tomb had waited thousands of years for Howard Carter to open it.

Activity

Imagine that you, like Howard Carter, have found an ancient tomb full of marvelous things. Write a firsthand account of how you found the tomb, how you opened it, and what you did with the wonderful things you found inside. Use your best descriptive ability, and don't forget to include your feelings about what you have done.

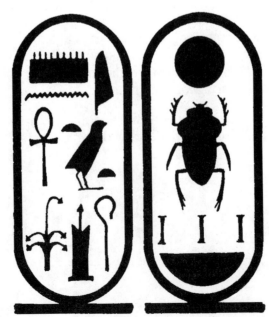

The Cartouche of King Tutankhamen

Quiz Time!

1. On the back of this paper list three important events in Section 4.

2. How did Ranofer figure out when Gebu must be doing his stealing?

    _____

3. To what innocent question did Gebu react violently? _____

    _____

4. What did Ranofer find, and how did he find it? _____

    _____

5. How did Ranofer handle the problem of the broken seal? _____

    _____

6. What new problem did Ranofer have after he found the goblet in Gebu's room?

    _____

7. Why was Ranofer upset when he saw Gebu leave in the morning with a bundle of shentis

    under his arm? _____

    _____

8. What feast day was coming soon, and why were Ranofer and Heqet excited about it?

    _____

9. How was Ranofer acting differently than usual with Heqet? _____

    _____

10. What did Heqet overhear? _____

    _____

Let's Make Jewelry

If you ever get to visit a museum with a large Egyptian exhibit, such as the British Museum in London, or the Rosicrucian Egyptian Museum in San Jose, California, you'll notice many exhibits of jewelry. Although much of the jewelry of the pharaohs was of gold and silver with precious or semi-precious stones, other jewelry was similar to much of what might be worn today.

Beads were very popular, and many necklaces, rings, and bracelets were made with beads of *faience,* an earthenware material with a tin glaze. Sometimes the faience beads were used alone, and at other times they were combined with glass beads or beads of different kinds of stones. Most of the faience beads are blue, while the glass beads are many different colors and resemble small American Indian beads.

It is easy to make beads of papíer-mâché which look very much like the original faience ones.

Materials:

- Strips of newspaper $^3/_8$ to $^1/_2$ inch (1 to 1.27 cm) wide and 2 inches (5 cm) long

- Wallpaper paste

- Fine wire, greased or oiled

- Thread or fine fishing line for stringing

- Tempera paint in slightly differing shades of blue

- Spray acrylic (Use only under the supervision of an adult.)

- Glass beads, if desired

Directions:

1. Dip strips of paper one at a time into wallpaper paste, then wind tightly around greased wire. Shape the wire with your fingers into a bead shape. Let dry.

2. Paint and let dry.

3. Spray very lightly with acrylic, so as not to close holes at ends of beads. Let dry.

4. Remove from wire.

5. String alone or with glass beads.

Note: A variation on making papíer–mâché beads involves using wallpaper in different colors and patterns. If you use wallpaper, you will not need to paint your beads, but you will need to put on a glossy coat of acrylic.

Decorate Your Tomb

Tutankhamen's tomb, as well other tombs which have been found in Egypt, have walls covered with beautifully colored pictures of what was important to the pharaoh. Some of the paintings are very graceful and relaxed ones of Tutankhamen and his wife in their daily life. Others show the pharaoh as it was imagined he would be in the afterlife. In the picture below, which is in the burial chamber, he is shown in three different ways: dressed as Osiris; standing before the sky goddess, Nut; and with Osiris, who is welcoming him as he is followed by his spirit double. (The gods and goddesses are described on page 45.)

On a separate sheet of plain paper, draw pictures of you in your life with the things and people who are important to you, then color your pictures in bright colors. You may include any words, names, or phrases which have meaning to you, as well as any symbols of you and your life.

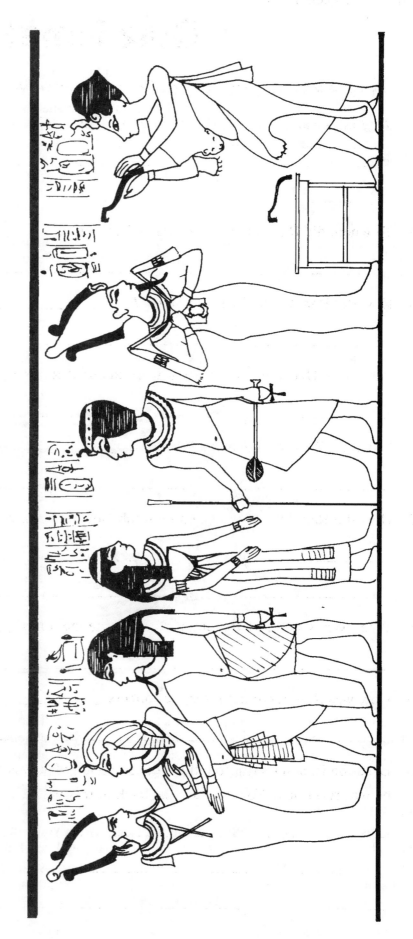

Fill a Time Capsule

Sometimes when a large new office building is first built, the owners will place a "time capsule" inside part of a wall. Inside the time capsule they place various items which seem to them to be typical of the current life of people in that area. The idea behind doing such a thing is to enable someone fifty or a hundred years later, or whenever the building is demolished, to see what was important to the people who built the building. They might enclose a newspaper, books, announcements, or pictures of the people involved with the building.

In a very real sense, the tomb of Tutankhamen was a marvelous time capsule, because for three thousand years it held more things than modern man had ever before seen representing the life of the pharaoh during a glorious period in Egypt's history. The lovely furniture, jewelry, pictures, statues of the gods, game boards, vases, model boats, shrines, thrones, musical instruments, and the magnificent coffins were almost entirely as they were when they were intended to go with the pharaoh into his afterlife.

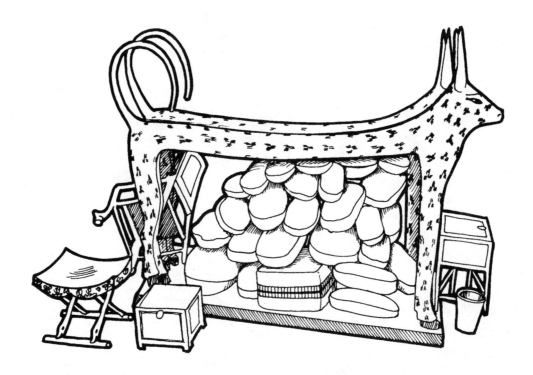

Because of these "wonderful things," as Howard Carter called them when he first saw them, and because of the beautiful pictures of Egyptian life during Tutankhamen's rule which also filled the tomb, we are now able to have a glimpse of what life was like for the pharaoh when he was alive which we would never have had otherwise. A little of the mystery of ancient Egypt was solved when we were able to see these things, or pictures of them, because the people in pictures then became real-life persons living and going about their business, teaching us three thousand years after their lives ended.

Activity

In groups of three or four, prepare a time capsule of what you would like people in the year 2100 to know about you and your life as it is now. Your space will be limited, so you must use it carefully, placing in it only items which seem to you to be most representative of your life today. Everyone in the group must agree on which items to include. After your time capsule is completed, report back to the class, explaining each item and its purpose in the capsule.

Writing Dialogue

Eloise McGraw is a writer who often uses dialogue to carry forward the action of her story. The skill of writing dialogue (conversation between two or more persons) is a very important skill to develop that will improve your writing. With good dialogue, you can accomplish several things in your story or essay. Effective characterization, for example, depends to a large extent on what the character says and what the other characters say about, or to, him or her. Just as you can tell a lot about a person by what he says, how he says it, and how other people react to what he says, you can tell a lot about a character in the same way.

Writing dialogue is not difficult. First, you'll need to "hear" the conversation in your head. What does each character say, and how does he say it? What does another character reply, and how does the other character react?

Then you need to remember two simple rules for writing dialogue: each time a different character speaks, you start a new paragraph, and you enclose exactly what a character says in quotation marks. Notice the following example which took place in a gas station:

> *"What do you think you're doing?" the burly man shouted as he climbed out of the giant-wheeled four-by-four. "Can't you see you're supposed to go in the other direction?"*
>
> *Carrie sat immobile in her car for a moment before answering. Obviously this man was very angry, although she wasn't sure what she'd done to cause such a reaction. "I don't see any arrows pointing one way or another," she finally answered.*
>
> *This only enraged the man more, and he advanced toward her menacingly. "If you don't watch out, I'll run this truck right over that little car of yours!"*
>
> *"Is that a threat?" Carrie retorted, looking straight into the man's eyes.*
>
> *"No," he backed down, "but you women ought to start learning how to drive better!"*

In this conversation, you are not given any physical details about either of the characters except that the man is burly, but you can tell a great deal about their personalities by what they say, can't you? The man is belligerent, loud, loses his temper easily, and doesn't seem to like women very much, but he backs right down as soon as he is confronted. The woman, on the other hand, is thoughtful, waits before she speaks, and is straightforward.

Sometimes, as in this conversation, you can actually show more of your character's personality by what he or she says and does than you might have been able to show with a physical description.

Activity

Picture a conversation between two people. Imagine the words that flow between them, what they are and how they are spoken. Then write the dialogue which you have imagined, remembering to observe the two rules of writing dialogue. You may wish to first write an introductory paragraph to provide the setting.

Make a Decision

Some readers might disagree with the way Ranofer handled the problems in his life and the way he handled Gebu. Do you think he did the right thing? Or do you think he might have handled things differently?

Not every decision in life is easy to make, and there is more than one way to solve most problems, some better than others. Sometimes it helps to sit down and make up two lists. On one list you include positives, and on the other you include negatives.

In the columns below list under "The Right Way" the actions Ranofer took which you think were good ones for him to take, and under "The Wrong Way" list the actions you think could have been better, if handled differently. You and your classmates will come back together to discuss the ideas each of you have, so be prepared to justify your decisions and offer other solutions, if necessary.

The Right Way	**The Wrong Way**

Any Questions?

When you finished reading *The Golden Goblet,* did you have some questions that were left unanswered? Write some of your questions here.

_____

_____

_____

_____

_____

- Work in groups or by yourself to prepare possible answers for some of the questions you have asked above and those written below. When you have finished your predictions, share your ideas with the class.

- What kind of adult did Ranofer grow up to be? Was he a successful goldsmith? Did he make jewelry for the queen's tomb? Did he make any of the beautiful things found in King Tutankhamen's tomb? Did he and Heqet work together as adults? Did Ranofer ever get his own gold-working shop?

- Was Ranofer around when Gebu and Wenamon were punished for grave robbing? When Ranofer grew to be a man, did he continue to believe he did the right thing about Gebu, or did he have second thoughts? Did the Ancient ever stop asking him whether he had seen any hangings lately?

- Who was the queen? Did she become famous as queen, or did she go on to be the mother of a famous pharaoh? How did she feel about the pharaoh's being able to have more than one wife? Was she jealous, or did she accept it as being just the way things were then? What did she really think about Ranofer's request for a donkey?

- How long did Ranofer's donkey live? Did he ever get another one later on? After he became a goldsmith, did he move back into town? Did very many Egyptian boys own donkeys, or was that a very unusual thing to do then?

- What kind of life did he lead as an adult? What did he do besides make things of gold? Did he go on to have a family? What was family life like for the common people in Egypt then? Did commoners sometimes marry their sisters, as the pharaohs did?

- Did Heqet also become a famous goldsmith? What kind of life did he lead, and did he and Ranofer remain partners and friends as adults?

Book Report Ideas

Books may be reported on in many ways. After reading *The Golden Goblet*, choose one of the following suggestions to use for your report, or you may use an idea of your own.

- **Be a Travel Agent**

  Pretend to be a travel agent in ancient Egypt. Prepare a poster advertising your favorite place and write the spiel you would give to prospective clients, urging them to go there on your tour. Give your spiel as an oral presentation to the class.

- **Be a Tour Guide**

  Pretend to be a tour guide who takes tourists to places of interest along the Nile. Write the script you would use, telling your tourists about the many sights they are seeing and a little of the history of each, then take the class on an imaginary tour.

- **Be a Tourist**

  Pretend to be a twelve-year-old boy from Greece who is seeing Egypt for the first time in about the year 500 B.C. Write a diary about your travels.

- **Make a Model**

  Using a map as a guide, and papíer–mâché or clay for materials, make a model of The Valley of the Kings or of the Nile Delta.

- **Script it!**

  In a size-appropriate group, write a script of one of the scenes from *The Golden Goblet* and present your dramatization of the script to the class. Costumes will make your presentation more realistic, but are not necessary.

- **Interview a Character**

  Do this with another student. One person takes the part of a character from the book and really steeps himself in what he sees to be the character's personality. The other person pretends to be a television interviewer. Interviewing requires some skill, and it is important to ask meaningful questions.

- **Make a Doll**

  Using either a figure of a human being which you have made yourself or a small character doll which you have gotten at a hobby shop, dress your doll as he or she would have been dressed during Ranofer's times. If you set the doll into a diorama setting, it will be more effective. You may even use more than one doll to portray a scene from the book.

- **Riddle, Riddle, Who Knows a Riddle?**

  Write a series of riddles about characters or scenes from the book, and ask them of the class. This could be turned into a contest or a game to see who could answer the largest number of riddles.

Research Ideas

Describe three things you read in *The Golden Goblet* that you would like to learn more about.

1. _____

2. _____

3. _____

As you read *The Golden Goblet*, you encountered many lifestyles, ways of speaking, beliefs, customs, unfamiliar words, and geographical locations which were new to you. Knowing more about ancient Egypt and its people, where they lived and what they believed will help you to understand the book more. Fortunately, the Egyptians left behind much fascinating information which we can study.

Work in groups to research one or more of the areas you named above or the areas that are listed below. Share what you learn with the rest of the class in any format that is appropriate for an oral presentation.

- Mummies
- Chariots
- The Nile
- Hieroglyphics
- Egyptian clothing
- Goldsmithing
- Life in the Pharaoh's palace
- Memphis
- Valley of the Kings
- The Great Pyramid
- Slavery in ancient Egypt
- Moses
- Stone quarries
- Crocodiles
- Egyptian family life
- Egyptians cosmetics
- Ptah
- Hieratic writing
- Osiris
- King Tutankhamen
- Cleopatra
- The Rosetta Stone
- Howard Carter
- Alexander the Great
- Archaeology
- Trade
- Pyramid of Chephren
- Kush

- Pyramids
- The Sphinx
- Pharaohs
- Scribes
- Glass
- Temple life
- Thebes
- The Nile Delta
- Temple of Karnak
- Step pyramids
- Egyptian wildlife
- Papyrus
- Egyptian boats
- Sarcophagus
- Mirrors
- Amon
- Bes
- Egyptian pottery
- Egyptian games
- Akhenaton
- The Middle Kingdom
- Abu Simbel
- Ptolemy
- Ramses II
- Book of the Dead
- Romans
- Nubians
- Hittites

Festival of the Nile

It's time to celebrate! We have just finished a wonderful new book and learned many fascinating things about the ancient civilization of the Egyptians. We've followed Ranofer through his daily life and read about what he believed. We've sympathized with him as he was treated badly, and we have rejoiced when he was able to free himself of what was a life of virtual slavery under his cruel half-brother and start on the way to becoming what he wanted to be. What better way to complete our study of Egypt than with a festival to commemorate what we've accomplished! We will call our festival "The Festival of the Nile" just as Ranofer's was called.

In many ways, life was much simpler during Ranofer's time than it is for us today. There were no machines, automobiles, microwave ovens, or televisions as we have now. People had to spend much of their time working hard for food, shelter, and clothing. They did not have the leisure time that we have or the opportunity to travel or to obtain an education. Food was much more basic and more apt to be prepared easily in Ranofer's time because, unless you had servants to wait on you, you did not have a lot of time to spend on cooking.

To plan your classroom Festival of the Nile, get together in small groups and use the Brainstorm Sheet on page 39. Follow the outline, then choose a spokesperson to report your ideas back to the class.

If you wish to invite others to your festival, use the invitation on page 40. Fill in the information using a calligraphy pen or marker. Add your cartouche or favorite design. Roll the invitation, as a scroll would be rolled. Drip melted wax onto the seam and press your "seal" onto the wax, then hand-deliver your invitation.

Here are some ideas for the displays and events from your Festival of the Nile:

Displays

- Readers' Response Journals
- Timeline of ancient Egypt to the present
- Pyramids
- Personal symbols
- Funeral masks
- Jewelry
- Stories of "The Mummy's Curse"
- Tomb designs
- Research work
- Foods typical of those Ranofer ate
- Books about ancient Egypt showing pictures of Tutankhamen's tomb and other Egyptian wonders
- Hieroglyphics

Events

- Demonstration of how the pyramids were built
- Demonstration of breaking the code of the hieroglyphics
- Narration of the finding of Tutankhamen's tomb
- Demonstration of how mummies were made
- Seal the time capsule and place somewhere in the school to be opened at a later time
- Feast on foods Ranofer might have eaten
- Panel discussion about what the Egyptians believed and how they lived

Brainstorm Sheet

Each small group should have a copy of this page to use for the activity described on page 38.

Brainstorm Sheet

Title for the Day _____

_____

_____

Who to Invite _____

_____

_____

What to Do _____

_____

_____

What to Display _____

_____

_____

Order of Events for the Day _____

_____

_____

Necessary Preparations _____

_____

_____

Invitation

Festival of the Nile

Please join us as we celebrate the completion of our unit on The Golden Goblet with a Festival of the Nile.

Day: _____

Time: _____

Place: _____

Presented by: _____

Conversations

Work in size-appropriate groups to write and perform the conversation that might have occurred in one of the following situations. If you prefer, you may use your own conversation idea for characters from *The Golden Goblet.*

- Thutra's spirit visits Ranofer, and they discuss the problems of what to do about Gebu's using Ranofer to steal.

- Heqet tells Rekh that Ibni is stealing gold by taking it out in the wineskin, and they discuss how to deal with him in a way which won't jeopardize Ranofer.

- Ranofer breaks down and tells Heqet and the Ancient about his life with Gebu.

- Gebu and Wenamon plan what they are going to do with the golden goblet.

- Ranofer and the Ancient discuss capital punishment.

- Ranofer testifies in court about the golden goblet and is cross-examined.

- Ranofer talks with Zau about how he has reshaped his life so he can become Zau's pupil.

- The Ancient and Heqet discuss with Ranofer whether it is right or wrong for him to report Gebu to the authorities.

- The Ancient and Ranofer talk about why the Ancient always says, "Been to any hangings lately?"

- Qa-Nefer and Ranofer discuss what it is like to be the favorite pet of the queen.

- Gebu and Wenamon talk about what they are going to do when they escape from the tomb.

- The soldiers confront Gebu and Wenamon emerging from the tomb.

- The guards report to the queen how they have handled Gebu and Wenamon.

- The queen asks Ranofer's help in planning ways to prevent thieves from entering the tombs in the Valley of the Kings in the future.

- Ranofer tells his son about his adventure in the Valley of the Tombs.

- Thutra appears in a dream to discuss what Ranofer saw in the palace.

- Ranofer, the Ancient, and Heqet recount their adventure on the day of the Festival of the Nile.

- The Ancient and Heqet help Ranofer plan his house in the desert.

- At the following Festival of the Nile, Ranofer, Heqet, and the Ancient recount the previous festival day and discuss the differences between then and now.

- Ranofer describes the palace for Heqet.

- Ranofer presents his first gold necklace to the queen, who remembers him.

Sample Journal Questions

Chapter 1   How is Ranofer's job in the goldshop different from the apprentice's job he wishes for?

Why is Gebu allowing Ranofer to work in the goldshop. What can Ranofer do about it?

Chapter 2   How did Ranofer meet the Ancient?

Describe the encounter between Ranofer and Gebu when Ranofer reveals he knows what is in the wineskin.

Chapter 3   Pretending to be Ranofer, tell of something you know how to do which most other boys you know in Egypt do not know.

What important job did Rekh entrust to Ranofer, and how did Ranofer complete it?

How did Gebu react when Ranofer arrived home without the wineskin?

Chapter 4   How does Ranofer dispose of the larger than usual breakfast Gebu left for him?

Do you think Ranofer will be able to trust Heqet? How can you tell?

Chapter 5   How do the Egyptians feel about someone who would rob a tomb?

What will Gebu do to Ranofer when he no longer brings home the wineskin?

Chapter 6   Compare Ranofer's treatment in the goldshop with that in Gebu's stonecutting shop.

Pretending to be Pai, describe your new apprentice, Ranofer.

What is the nocturnal mystery which sometimes awakens Ranofer in the night?

Chapter 7   How do Heqet and Ranofer plan for Ranofer to continue learning how to work gold?

Why does Ranofer dig a lotus root on the way to meet Heqet?

Chapter 8   Describe the conversation between Zau and Ranofer.

What can Ranofer tell Gebu about the coppers?

Chapter 9   How can Ranofer learn what Gebu is doing to get rich?

Why is Ranofer afraid of the dark?

Chapter 10   What did Ranofer ask which sent Gebu into a rage?

How did Ranofer discover where Gebu was getting his newfound wealth?

Chapter 11   How will Gebu react if he learns of what Ranofer has done?

What is different about Gebu's behavior to Ranofer now?

Chapter 12   What happened to the golden goblet?

What is significant about the broken tree?

Chapter 13   Why did Ranofer fall into the tomb?

How did Heqet and the Ancient figure out where Ranofer had gone?

Chapter 14   Describe the room Ranofer found himself in, in the tomb.

How does Ranofer feel as he is leaving the tomb and why?

Chapter 15   How does Ranofer get into the palace?

Who comes to Ranofer's rescue?

Chapter 16   How does the queen test Ranofer to see whether or not he is telling the truth?

What reward does Ranofer ask for and get, and what happens to Gebu?

Gods and Goddesses of Ancient Egypt

Religion was very important to the ancient Egyptians, and they had many gods and goddesses. But they did not have a religion which stayed the same throughout the 3,000 or so years of their civilization. New interpretations of the gods and new symbols were continually being formed as historical or political influences changed, with each interpretation or symbol being considered as just one aspect of the truth. Because of this, the importance of one god as compared to another, or even what each symbolized, also changed over the years. Early on, each city had its own god.

The principal gods and goddesses who were worshipped over many years included the following:

Amon King of the gods; patron deity of the pharaohs; identified with the sun god Re as Amon-Re. He was pictured as a male figure with a ram's head or a ram wearing a triple crown.

Ptah God of fertility and creator of the universe; god of Memphis and patron god of craftsmen. He was pictured as a mummified man with a shaved head.

Osiris Originally, he was a fertility god; later with Re, he became the supreme god of Egypt and ruler of the dead. He was pictured as a dead king in mummy wrappings with his hands holding the crook and flail and wearing a crown on his head.

Re (Ra) Personification of the sun at its zenith; king of the gods and father of mankind; protector of kings and chief state god. He was pictured as a falcon-headed man crowned with the sun disk and holding the ankh and a scepter.

Horus Originally the god of Lower Egypt and later identified with the reigning pharaoh. He was pictured as a falcon or falcon-headed male figure.

Thoth Moon god. Later he was the god of learning, inventor of writing, scribe of the gods, and the lord of magic.

Tefnut Goddess of life-giving dew and moisture, and protectress of Osris. She helped to support the sky, and when her tears fell to the ground, they were said to turn into incense-bearing plants. She was pictured as a lioness or with the head of a lion.

Nut Goddess of the sky; arch of the heavens; protectress of the dead. She is pictured as an elongated female figure arched over Shu and wore a water-pot on her head.

Mut Vulture goddess of Thebes, a great divine mother. She was pictured with the head of a vulture or with a headdress in the form of a vulture.

Isis (Eset) Queen of the gods; great mother goddess figure; embalmer of the body of Osiris and protector of the child Horus. She is pictured as a female figure with a vulture headdress and a throne or disk flanked by cow's or ram's horns on her head.

Seth (Set) Partner and rival of Horus; murderer of Osiris. Most of the time, Seth was not in favor as a god, and he was pictured as being associated with pigs, boars, hippopotamuses, crocodiles and serpents. He is pictured with the Typhonian head on human shoulders.

Bibliography

Resource and Reference Materials

Allen, Tony. *The Time Traveller Book of Pharaohs and Pyramids.* EDC Publishing, 1992.

Boase, Wendy. *Ancient Egypt.* Gloucester Press, 1978.

Davis, Kenneth C. *Don't Know Much About Geography.* William Morrow and Company, 1992.

Edwards, I.E.S. *Treasures of Tutankhamen.* Ballantine Books, 1978.

Halliburton, Richard. *Book of Marvels.* Bobbs-Merrill Company, Inc., 1960.

Houston, James D. *Writing from the Inside.* Addison-Wesley Publishing Company, Inc., 1973.

Ions, Veronica. *Egyptian Mythology.* Paul Hamlyn, 1968.

Milton, Joyce. *Secrets of the Mummies.* Random House, 1984.

Rosicrucian Egyptian Museum. *The Egyptian Alphabet.* 1990.

Schar, Grant. *Making Mummies.* Rosicrucian Egyptian Museum, 1991.

Other Historical Fiction

Buck, Pearl S. *The Good Earth.* Pocket Books, Simon & Schuster, 1958.

Collier, James Lincoln and Christopher Collier. *My Brother Sam Is Dead.* Scholastic Inc., 1974.

Forbes, Esther. *Johnny Tremain.* Dell Publishing Group, Inc., 1987.

Gray, Elizabeth Janet. *Adam of the Road.* Scholastic Inc., 1970.

Houston, Jeane Wakatsuki and James D. Houston. *Farewell to Manzanar.* Bantam Pathfinder Editions, 1983.

Keith, Harold. *Rifles for Watie.* Harper & Row Junior Books, 1991.

McGraw, Eloise. *The Striped Ships.* Margaret K. McElderry Books, Macmillan Publishing Company, 1991.

O'Dell, Scott. *Sing Down the Moon.* Dell Publishing Group, Inc., 1970.

Sheredy, Kate. *The Singing Tree.* Scholastic, Inc., 1967.

Speare, Elizabeth George. *The Witch of Blackbird Pond.* A Yearling Book, Dell Publishing Co. Inc., 1958.

Yates, Elizabeth. *Amos Fortune Free Man.* Puffin Books, Viking Penguin, 1989.

Answer Key

Page 10

1. Accept all appropriate responses.
2. Thutra; goldsmith
3. Thebes
4. Because of his servility; his cheese-white hands with dirty nails, stained teeth; his slimy questionability.
5. Accept answers which show understanding that the people believed in many gods and the expressions reflected their beliefs.
6. Accept all appropriate answers.
7. To read and write
8. Shares his food; confides in him; wants to help him
9. To make gold leaves for a necklace
10. Accept answers which show understanding that Gebu was using Ranofer to steal and that was the only reason he would keep him.

Page 15

1. Accept appropriate responses.
2. The goldsmith for whom Ranofer works.
3. Because of the story Heqet told him of how his father was able to trust him with valuable things in the storehouse.
4. Put it into the wineskin for Ranofer to carry to Gebu.
5. Heqet told him; he waited a few days, then fired Ibni.
6. Death by hanging upside down by one foot
7. Accept appropriate responses.
8. He made him an apprentice in the stonecutting shop.
9. They were deformed from years of stonecutting.
10. Accept appropriate responses.

Page 17, Answer to Code,

Language is fun!

Page 20

1. Accept appropriate responses.
2. Stone coffins and sarcophagi
3. He said it was noisy, gritty, altogether horrid, the foreman was a living wasps' nest, the other apprentice, a stupid nobody.
4. Because he does not want to accept food from Heqet.
5. Because it is a good trade and it's better to have that trade than none at all.
6. To the shop of Zau, the goldsmith.
7. Ranofer's father was his old friend. He thought that Ranofer had shown talent for working with gold as a young boy, and he's willing to take him on as a pupil free, if Ranofer can reshape his life.
8. He was beaten.
9. Stealing again
10. To spy on Gebu, Wenamon, and Setma.

Page 25

1. Accept appropriate answers.
2. He figured that was the only reason Gebu would be going out after dark, because what he wanted more than anything was gold.
3. Asking about the purpose of a little room on the scroll plan of a tomb.
4. A golden goblet; he sneaked into Gebu's room when Gebu was gone and found it.
5. He sneaked back into the room, scraped the crumbs of dry mud into a little pile, then dampened them and put them back onto the seal.
6. How to tell someone about Gebu's stealing without himself being thought guilty.
7. Because Ranofer had planned to take the goblet, and he realized that Gebu had it.
8. The Festival of the Nile. There would be a feast and no work.
9. He was very quiet, very serious and kept changing the subject.
10. Gebu and Wenamon planning to meet at the broken tree.

Answer Key *(cont.)*

Page 30

1. Accept appropriate responses.
2. Because he loved the pharaoh and the gods of Egypt and because he wanted to be free.
3. To the Valley of the Tombs.
4. A vulture flew out of the hole which led down into the tomb, startling Ranofer so that he fell in. Once in, he decided to follow Gebu and Wenamon to see what they were doing.
5. Because he was supposed to meet them, and they thought he would not have passed up the free food, they set out to find him.
6. Furniture decorated with gold, alabaster honey jars, painted wooden boxes, wicker trunk, winecups, scent jars, and jeweled collars and arm bands; many other things, all arranged to look as though they were in a beautiful home.
7. By the cartouches
8. Robbing it
9. He pushed the stone over the top of the hole, and the Ancient and Heqet sat on it to keep Gebu and Wenamon from getting out.
10. Accept appropriate responses with extra credit for including the test the queen gave Ranofer to see whether or not he was lying.

Page 41
Matching

1. g
2. h
3. j
4. i
5. a
6. d
7. e
8. c
9. k
10. l
11. f
12. b

True or False

1. False
2. True
3. True
4. False
5. True

Short Answer

1. Ibni, the Babylonian.
2. He had plenty to eat, was learning to be a goldsmith, and was treated well with Thutra; with Gebu he had little to eat, he was apprenticed to be a stone cutter, and he was beaten often.
3. They caused Ranofer to realize that Gebu was doing his thievery at night.
4. To the Valley of the Tombs and into a tomb.
5. He climbed up onto a ledge.

Essay

Accept all appropriate responses. Give extra credit for the use of dialogue.